WHEN YOU PRAY
NOT
IF

SARAH MORGAN

Copyright © Sarah Morgan
ISBN 978-1-5136-5879-7

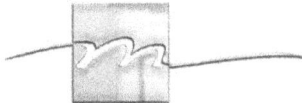

MORGAN PUBLISHING
The Pen of a Ready Writer

When You Pray Not If

Published by Morgan Publishing
888-320-5622

Join the Movement, and Connect with us on:
www.prayeracademy.university
www.prayeracademyglobal.com
www.facebook.com/prayeracademyglobal
www.instagram.com/prayeracademyglobal
www.twitter.com/prayeracademy

DEDICATION

This series of books is dedicated to the thousands of Prayer Academy Students across this nation, the Prayer Altar Call family, and the countless elite warriors, intercessors, travailing women, and warring men. The Bible says, *"The generous will prosper; those who refresh others will themselves be refreshed" (Proverbs 11:25, NIV).* As you have energized, restored, and revived others through your intercession, may you experience a wind of refreshing blowing over you in the place of PRAYER— the place of POWER!

Yours Truly,
Sarah Morgan

PREFACE

HOW TO USE THIS BOOK

The Prayer Declaration Series is designed to strengthen your relationship with God by gaining an awareness of the importance of engaging in prayer for tangible results.

Effective prayer will cause you to soar like an eagle in God's plan for your life. It is a vital key to tapping into the wisdom of God, which will elevate you above mediocrity to produce astounding exploits to the Glory of God.

> *"But the people who know their God shall prove themselves strong and shall stand firm and do exploits [for God]"* (Daniel 11:32).

An intimate prayer life will stabilize and secure every area of your life. Contrary to some opinions, prayer should not be boring. Prayer should be the highlight of your day. Albeit, there is no set way to pray; there are guidelines:

1. Pray to God, the Father, in the name of Jesus Christ.
2. Seek to Establish a Good Personal Relationship with the Lord.
3. Make Sure Your Prayers Always Line Up With the Perfect Will of God for Your Life.
4. Back-Up Your Prayers with Specific Scripture Verses.
5. Do not be Afraid to Write Your Prayers Out to the Lord.
6. Do not be Afraid to go into *Prevailing* Prayer, as Lead by the Holy Spirit.
7. Ask the Holy Spirit to Help You with Your Prayer Life (Romans 8:26).
8. Ask Others to Pray in Agreement with You When Needed.
9. Always Include Prayers of Thanksgiving.
10. Start with Early Morning Prayer and Keep an Ear Tuned to the Holy Spirit Throughout the Entire Day.
11. Read and use the Prayers/Confessions found in the Prayer Declaration Series.

12. Pray in the Holy Spirit. If You have Received the Gift of the Holy Spirit (the language of the Spirit), you can receive it today. If You Have not received Him, ask; He will fill you. The Gift is Free!

13. Confess Scriptures Straight from the Word.

14. Pray a Scripture from the Word and Expand upon that Prayer, Spontaneously.

15. Pray the Word that is Hidden/Planted in your Heart, Spontaneously.

16. Receive Specific Guidance from the Holy Spirit as to What and How to Pray the Word.

17. Meditate on What You Read From Scripture and Pray the Word from Memory.

18. Pray God's Word and in Your Heavenly Language, and Alternate as the Spirit Leads.

Finally, have a great hunger for God—desperation to pray His will and submit to Him from your heart/spirit. Allow the Holy Spirit to search you. Then, be diligent in crucifying your flesh. Do not be satisfied with self-directed prayer; dig deep into the spirit realm.

When you allow the Holy Spirit to lead you, your spirit will issue, out the forces of life, with effectual fervent prayer. Continue to press into the spirit realm, until your spiritual antennas' tune in to the promptings and leadings of the Holy Spirit. Then as you speak, every stronghold is destroyed, and the power of God released.

When you press into the place of prayer, in the spirit, your spirit becomes one with the Spirit of God. Then, you will pray His desires from your heart, and become intimate with Him, commune with Him, and become lost in Him. It is at that moment; your mind is in total subjection to pray the will of the Father.

Prayer is not forceful but flowing. Prayer is such a great joy that you cannot get enough. May the Spirit of Grace and Supplication fill you to overflowing in the *place of prayer*.

HOW TO ENTER INTO A TIME OF PRAYER

A.C.T

A - Acknowledge Him for Who He is.

"Know ye that the LORD He is God: it is He that hath made us, and not we ourselves; we are His people, and the sheep of His pasture" (Psalms 100:3).

C – Confess Your Sins, Faults, and Shortcomings.

"If we say that we have no sin, we deceive ourselves, and the truth is not in us. If we confess our sins, he is faithful and just to forgive us our sins, and to cleanse us from all unrighteousness" (1 John 1:8-9).

T - Thanksgiving

"Enter into his gates with thanksgiving, and into his courts with praise be thankful unto him, and bless his name" (Psalms 100:4).

CONTENTS

ACKNOWLEDGMENTS

First, to my Abba Father, Pater, Provider, Protector, Preserver, to His Son Jesus and to precious Holy Spirit, my Senior Partner, without this Terrific Trio, I can do nothing. I am eternally grateful and privileged to serve and committed to the cause.

Karla Allen, thank you for editing, formatting, proofing, and helping expedite the process of production. You are a blessing to your generation. I appreciate you.

Sarah Morgan

WHEN YOU PRAY NOT IF

WHEN YOU PRAY NOT IF

INTRODUCTION

SOME FUNDAMENTAL TRUTHS ABOUT PRAYER:

There are no easy prayers – praying is not idle chit-chat; it is a decisive effort to communicate how you feel to God, and a desperate attempt to hear God respond. That doesn't happen by default, it is by you and I being intentional in our approach in prayer.

"The Bible is Our Prayer Book."

It teaches us how to pray – every chapter of every Book in the Bible shows us our need for reliance on God instead of on ourselves.

Better than that even, it teaches us about how to get answers to prayer – how to obtain what we need, on a moment by moment basis.

Prayer is not an act that you just do, but rather an interaction, with God, that unlocks what you need!

Remember, anything that is not birthed through prayer is illegal.

- Prayer is a birth canal. It creates and establishes a place for God to cultivate and nurture holiness, righteousness, purity, and Godly character in us.

- Prayer creates an atmosphere where everyone carries a spirit of prayer, not just a belief of prayer but the behavior of prayer, a conviction of prayer, a mantle of prayer.
- Prayer can stop things.
- Prayer stretches and creates openings that enable us to birth the will and purpose of God in the earth.
- Prayer brings you to a place where you partner with God. You establish a divine relationship, which makes you a co-creator and a co-controller in the universe with Him.
- Prayer influences what happens on earth. When earth prays, heaven responds. If nothing leaves earth, nothing leaves heaven.
- Prayer is something that works. Prayer is powerful. Prayer is a deadly and effective weapon for destroying the works of the enemy.
- Prayer is stretching out with expectation and unleashing the power of God. Prayer reaches into another dimension and brings the Kingdom of God into your environment, situation, circumstances, your space, your home, your city, and your nation.
- Prayer breaks the cedars, divides the flames of

fire, and shakes the wilderness of Ka'desh- (Psalm 29:8).

- Prayer is a lifestyle, which translates and transfers us to another dimension and expression of his glory.
- Prayer establishes boundaries, borders, and parameters. Prayer pushes back evil spirits, entities, and despotisms.
- Prayer is standing, building, resisting, renouncing, forbidding, disallowing, decreeing, declaring, and establishing.
- Prayer is communion with God, which is a relationship from the heart to throne, spirit to spirit invading the impossible, and breaking human limitations.
- Prayer is standing in the gap, building up a hedge of protection and crying out to God. Prayer is stretching out with expectation and unleashing the power of God.
- Prayer is reaching into another dimension and bringing the Kingdom of God into your environment, situation, circumstances, your space, your home, city, nation, and your church.
- And it came to pass, that, as he was praying in a

certain place, when he ceased, one of his disciples said unto him, Lord teach us to pray, as John has also taught his disciples. And He said unto them, "When ye pray, SAY," which means prayer has a VOICE. You just can't think or imagine prayer; you must open your mouth and say something. - Luke 11:1-2

- But shall believe that those things which he saith shall come to pass; he shall have whatsoever he saith. Our Father which art in heaven, Hallowed be thy name. Thy kingdom come, Thy will be done, as in heaven, so in earth. - Mark 11:23b

- Powerful prayer is bringing in the Kingdom atmosphere; it's bringing the government of God into the environment.

- Prayer brings the power of God into a situation, region, church, community, and nation.

- Powerful prayer activates Isaiah 58:6 whereby you loose the bands of wickedness, undo the heavy burdens, let the oppressed go free and break every yoke.

- Powerful prayer breaks yokes of intimidation, manipulation, resistance, and opposition.

- Powerful prayer, dependent on God, generates

miracle-working energy.

- Have a mandate of prayer, a heart for prayer, and a passion for prayer!

Prayer, real prayer, is powerful and effective! It is THE most powerful act you will ever do, more than preaching, more than fighting, more than loving, and more than dying. Prayer is powerful!

THE WHEN FACTOR

We want to examine the WHEN factor of prayer, but before we do that, let's endeavor to understand the word "when" in its proper context. I am of the persuasion that understanding makes us outstanding.

The word "When" is commonly noted as an adverb, sometimes as a pronoun. In these instances, "When" denotes a pre-requisite. A prerequisite is a required prior condition. If something is required in advance of something else, a mandatory requirement is necessary. Also, we use" When" to refer to a future situation or condition that we are certain of, whereas we use *if* to introduce a possible or unreal situation.

So then "When" in this context denotes expectation and anticipation of a favorable outcome as a result of my fulfillment of the pre-requisite in prayer. Jesus, the Master teacher, taught the most powerful

"When's" you pray that guarantee an unprecedented response from heaven.

We will examine five pre-requisites and a few favorable outcomes or manifestations in this book.

The word if God is clear "WHEN" not "IF" you Pray, should you expect a response from heaven. Only "When" earth "Prays" does heaven respond.

CHAPTER 1

WHEN YOU PRAY, YOU ARE "NOT" TO BE LIKE THE HYPOCRITES.

*"But you, **When** you pray, you are not to be like the **hypocrites**; for they love to stand and pray in the synagogues and on the street corners so that they may be seen by men. Truly I say to you, they have their reward in full" (Matthew 6:5 NASB)*

Hypocrite - **(Easton's Bible Dictionary)**

1. One who puts on a mask and feigns himself to be what he is not; a dissembler in religion. Our Lord severely rebuked the scribes and Pharisees for their hypocrisy (Matt. 6:2, 5, 16). "*The hypocrite's hope shall perish*" (Job 8:13). The Hebrew word here rendered "***hypocrite***" rather means the "***godless***" or "***profane***," as it is rendered in Jeremiah 23:11 polluted with crimes.

Hypocrite - **(Webster's 1828 Dictionary)**

1. One who feigns or pretends to be what he is not, one who has the form of godliness without the power, or who assumes an appearance of piety and virtue, when he is destitute of true religion.

2. A dissembler, one who assumes a false appearance. One who is in-truthful, two-faced, has double standards.

Our prayers must not be characterized by behavior that contradicts what one claims to believe or feel. *"for they love to stand and pray in the synagogues and on the street corners so that they **may be seen by men**" (Matthew 6:5).*

> *"You're hopeless, you religion scholars and Pharisees! Frauds! You keep meticulous account books, tithing on every nickel and dime you get, but on the meat of God's Law, things like fairness and compassion and commitment—the absolute basics!—you carelessly take it or leave it. Careful bookkeeping is commendable, but the basics are required. Do you have any idea how silly you look, writing a life story that's wrong from start to finish, nitpicking over commas and semicolons" (Matthew 23:23-24, MSG)?*

"You blind Pharisee! First clean the inside of the cup and of the plate, so that the outside may be clean also. Woe to you, scribes and Pharisees, pretenders (hypocrites)! For you are like tombs that have been whitewashed, which look beautiful on the outside but inside are full of dead men's bones and everything impure. Just so, you also outwardly seem to people to be just and upright but inside you are full of pretense and lawlessness and iniquity" *(Matthew 23:26-28, AMP).*

For there is no faithfulness in their mouth; their inward part is very wickedness; their throat is an open sepulcher; they flatter with their tongue. (Psalms 5:9)

Our prayers must be characterized by integrity or fairness and straight/forwardness in conduct, thought, speech, etc.; upright; just; equitable; trustworthy; truthful; sincere; free from fraud, guile, or duplicity; not false; Without dissimulation; Without pretensions; Marked by truth.

"Behold, thou desirest truth in the inward parts: and in the hidden part thou shalt make

*me to know wisdom. Purge me with hyssop, and
I shall be clean: wash me, and I shall be whiter
than snow" (Psalm 51:6-7).*

"The hypocrite's hope shall perish" (Job 8:13).

In prayer, we create a climate of hope and expectation, and hope does not disappoint.

So "WHEN" we PRAY, let us not be like the Hypocrites in Jesus' Name.

PRAYER*: Father, In Jesus' name, I ask for forgiveness. If my prayers have been like those of the hypocrites, today, I receive the grace for my prayers to characterized by the integrity of heart, without dissimulation, without pretension and not for public* display and approval, but it will be acceptable in thy sight alone. Amen!

CHAPTER 2

WHEN YOU PRAY GO INTO YOUR "INNER" ROOM

*But you, **When** you pray, go into your Inner room, close your door and pray to your Father who is in secret, and your Father who sees what is done in secret will reward you" (Matthew 6:6, NASB).*

Inner - (Webster's 1828 Dictionary)

1. IN'NER, a. [from in.] Interior; farther inward than something else, as an inner chamber; the inner court of a temple or palace.

Another word for the Inner room is "*chamber.*"
Chamber - (Easton's Bible Dictionary)

2. To enter into a chamber is used metaphorically of prayer and communion with God.

*"Come, my people, enter thou into thy **chambers**, and shut thy doors about thee: hide thyself as it were for a little moment, until the indignation be over past" (Isaiah 26:20).*

*"And Elijah took the child, and brought him down out of the **chamber** into the house, and delivered him unto his mother: and Elijah said, See, thy son liveth"* (1 Kings 17:23).

*"Now when Daniel knew that the writing was signed, he went into his house; and his windows being open in his **chamber** toward Jerusalem, he kneeled upon his knees three times a day, and prayed, and gave thanks before his God, as he did aforetime"*
(Daniel 6:10).

These men assembled and found Daniel praying and making supplication before his God.

Another word for the *"Inner"* room is the *"Private room."*

*"But when you pray, go into your [most] **private room**, and, closing the door, pray to your Father, Who is in secret, and your Father, Who sees in secret, will reward you in the open"* *(Matthew 6:6, AMPC).*

1 . Not publicly known; not open; as a private negotiation. Communing with God in the private places of your heart.

Another word for the "Inner" room is the "Secret Place."

> *"But when you pray, go into your room, close the door and pray to your Father, who is unseen. Then your Father, who sees what is done in **secret**, will reward you" (Matthew 6:6).*

> *"He that dwelleth in the secret place of the most High shall abide under the shadow of the Almighty" (Psalms 91:1).*

Secret

1. Something studiously concealed. Removed from sight; private; unknown. *Abide in a secret place and hide thyself (I Samuel 19).*

2. That which is known to God only. *"Secret things belong to the Lord our God"* (Deuteronomy 29:29).

When we open the most intimate secrets of our heart to God in the "secret place," He who hears and sees in the "secret" will reward you in the open.

PRAYER: Father, In Jesus' name, today, I receive the grace for my prayers from my inner chambers of my heart to be sincere and pure in the privacy of Your presence.

Help me to be safely vulnerable, knowing that you have my best interest and will reward me publicly. Amen!

CHAPTER 3

WHEN YOU PRAY NO VAIN REPETITIONS

*"And **WHEN** you are praying, do not use meaningless **REPETITION** as the Gentiles do, for they suppose that they will be heard for their many words" (Matthew 6:7, NASB).*

Repetition

1. The repeated use of the same word or word pattern as a rhetorical device.

2. A rhetorical device is a use of language that creates a literary effect (but often without regard for literal significance.

3. Harp on, to dwell on tediously, to repeat endlessly and monotonously.

Now, vain repetition, therefore, cannot just mean repeating. It's VAIN repeating. Vain repetition. From the model prayer, we see that it can't just mean repeating because one of the greatest prayers in the Bible involved repetition. And, what He is condemning in Matthew 6:7 is this business about constant reciting of *"**Our Father which art in heaven, hallowed be thy name, thy kingdom come,**"* etc.--and then flip the beads around. "Our Father which art in heaven, hail, Mary, Mother of God, full of grace, Lord," unconsciously, ritualistically to the point that it loses meaning and essence; THAT is vain repetition. That's saying one prayer over and over and over and over and over VAINLY.

Jesus states, *"**Do not heap up empty phrases as the Gentiles do.**"* Note that He is talking about the Hebrew tradition of prayer (which quite obviously included much repetition, such as in the Psalms and priestly **chants and prayers** which could end up being empty and void of essence but become ritualistic.

PRAYER: Father, In Jesus' name, today, I receive the grace for my prayers not to become a rhetorical device as in use of language that creates a literary effect but often without regard for literal significance. I receive the grace not to harp on, to dwell on tediously, to repeat endlessly and monotonously, in my prayers. Instead, I will pray precisely, articulately, according to Your Word, knowing that You hear me, and You will answer me. Amen!

CHAPTER 4

WHEN YOU PRAY BELIEVE

"Therefore I say to you, whatever things you ask **WHEN** *you pray,* **BELIEVE** *that you receive them, and you will have them" (Mark 11:24, NKJV).*

Believe - (Webster's 1828 Dictionary)
Belie"ve

1. In theology, to believe sometimes expresses a mere assent of the understanding to the truths of the gospel, as in the case of Simon. Acts 8. In others, the word implies, with this assent of the mind, a yielding of the will and affections, accompanied by a humble reliance on Christ for salvation. John 1:12; 3:15.

2. It is to credit upon the authority or testimony of another, to be persuaded of the truth of something upon the declaration of another, or upon evidence furnished by reasons, arguments, and deductions

of the mind, or by other circumstances, than personal knowledge. When we believe upon the authority of another, we always put confidence in his veracity.

When we believe upon the authority of reasoning, arguments, or concurrence of facts and circumstances, we rest our conclusions upon their strength or probability, their agreement with our own experience.

"I had fainted, unless I had believed to see the goodness of the Lord in the land of the living" (Psalm 27:13).

Believing is to have a firm persuasion of anything. In some cases, to have full persuasion, approaching to certainty; in others, more doubt is implied. Believing is often followed by in or on, especially in the scriptures.

To **BELIEVE** *is to expect or hope with confidence; to trust.*

To **BELIEVE** in is to hold as the object of faith. *"Ye believe in God, believe also in me"* (John 14.1).

To **BELIEVE** on is to trust, to place full confidence in, to rest upon with faith.

"But, as many as received Him, To them gave He the power to become the sons of God, even to them that believe on His name" (John 1.12).

When you pray, you must **BELIEVE** on Him and **BELIEVE** in His Word.

PRAYER: *Father, in Jesus' name, today I receive the grace to believe on, to trust, to place full confidence in, to rest upon with faith in You and Your Word. As I stand praying, I expect and hope with confidence, trusting that I have and will receive whatever I ask for in faith, not doubting in my heart. Amen!*

CHAPTER 5

WHEN YOU PRAY, FORGIVE

*And **WHEN** ye stand praying, **FORGIVE**, if ye have an ought against any: that your Father also which is in heaven may forgive you your trespasses (Mark 11:25, KJV).*

Forgive - (Webster's 1828 Dictionary)

1. To pardon; to remit, as an offense or debt; to overlook an offense and treat the offender as not guilty. The original and proper phrase is to forgive the offense, to send it away, to reject it, that is, not to impute it, [put it to] the offender. But by a smooth transition, we also use the phrase, to forgive the person offending.

"Forgive us our debts. If we forgive men their trespasses, your Heavenly Father will also forgive you" (Matthew 6:12).

It is to be noted that pardon, like forgive, may be followed by the name or person, and by the offense, but

37

remit can be followed by the offense only. We forgive or pardon the man, but we do not remit him. (God will remit them of their sin.)

2 . To remit as a debt, fine, or penalty.

PRAYER: Father, In Jesus' name, today, I receive the grace to forgive, pardon, and release all those who have wronged and offended me so that You will forgive me. I overlook every offense and treat my offenders as not guilty as You have overlooked mine and released me from all guilt, that my prayers will be answered. Amen!

CHAPTER 6

WHEN YOU PRAY, SAY

*"So He said to them, "**WHEN** you pray, **SAY**: Our Father in heaven, Hallowed be Your name. Your kingdom come. Your will be done on earth as it is in heaven" (Luke 11:2, NKJV).*

Saying - (Webster's 1828 Dictionary)

1. Uttering inarticulate sounds or words; speaking; telling; relating; reciting.
2. An expression; a sentence uttered; a declaration.

Anything that must be said has to have a **VOICE**, which means prayer has a **VOICE**. **There are two main types of voice:** active voice and passive voice. The third type of voice called "middle" voice also exists but is less commonly used.

VOICE IS:

- The sound produced by the vocal organs of a vertebrate, especially a human.

- The ability to produce sounds:
- The mind as it produces verbal thoughts: *listening to the voice within.*

VOICE Creates SOUND.

VOICE Articulates vocabulary and language.

VOICE Carries Expression of Thought.

> *(Expression: utterance gives voice to your feelings).*

VOICE emphasis's the Expression through Tone, Volume, and Pitch. (Intensity)

Synonyms for VOICE

- Express, Air, Vent
- These verbs mean to give an outlet to thoughts or emotions.

VOICE denotes the verbal expression of an outlook or viewpoint:

VOICE is the sound made by the vibration of the vocal cords, especially when modified by the resonant effect of the tongue and mouth, which is called Speech.

"When you pray, SAY!"

So, you can't just stop at thinking or imagining a prayer; you have to say it to activate a response.

Speech:

1. The faculty or power of speaking; ability to express one's thoughts and emotions by speech sounds; the act of speaking; something that is spoken; an utterance; a form of communication in spoken language, made by a speaker.

Like everyday things in your home, your car, or on your person can be Voice activated.

- Light switches
- Thermostats
- Your car's guidance system.
- Cell phones [Siri]
- Recorders
- Watches
- Bluetooth's

Jesus was teaching a powerful prayer principle that guarantees a response from heaven, and that is prayer has a voice; hence your prayer voice activates the response.

PRAYER ACTIVATES GOD – JUST ASK

Can you comprehend the fact that we can activate the most Powerful, Holy, Glorious, Purest, and Loving Force in the world? *Your **VOICE** can activate God.* He is ready at a moment's notice to assist you. He is literally at your beck and call.

It is written in the Scriptures,

> *"I believed, so I spoke." Our faith is like this, too. We believe, and so we speak"*
> *(2 Corinthians 4:13, NCV).*

FAITH IS **VOICE** ACTIVATED:

> *"It is written in the Scripture, "I believed, so I spoke" (2 Corinthian*s 4:13, NCV).

- Our faith is like this, too. We believe, and so we **speak**.
- In the spiritual realm, your **VOICE** has power when you speak from the perspective of faith!
- God has set up a **VOICE** activation system of faith when our mouth is connected to our hearts.
- When we speak according to Scripture, we can possess those things that are promised to us.

- It was Jesus who said,

"When you pray believe that you receive, and you shall have it." Mark 11: 24

- **PRAYING INVOLVES SAYING SOMETHING!**
- This is giving **VOICE** to your faith!
- That is how our faith works.

"We believe, and therefore we speak"

(2 Corinthians 4:13).

As God's representative on the earth, He has given us the authority to speak for Him. When we speak under the leading of the Holy Spirit, we speak as His voice on the earth. During strategic times, the Lord will prompt us to pray prayers that will bring breakthrough." --

As His representatives on earth, we must learn to be His **VOICE** and speak clearly with His authority. Do we realize that we can become God's **VOICE** for breakthrough?

GOD'S MOUTHPIECE [*HE SHALL SPEAK FOR YOU TO THE PEOPLE; HE WILL ACT AS A MOUTHPIECE FOR YOU, AND YOU SHALL BE AS GOD TO HIM] (EXODUS 4:16, AMP).*

A mouthpiece is a piece or part, as of a musical instrument applied to or held in the mouth. A mouthpiece is also one who acts as a spokesperson on behalf of an organization. A mouthpiece does not act independently. The mouthpiece is vital in helping the musician produce the right sound. It is the conduit through which God's will is declared in the earth through prayer.

- We are the **VOICE** of the Lord on the earth as we positively declare His will through our prayers.
- God many times is waiting for something to be done on earth, but He needs someone to pray His will.
- Your **VOICE** matters.

As Mordecai told Esther when the Jews faced a terrible threat, "For if you remain completely **SILENT** at this time, relief and deliverance will arise for the Jews from another place, but you and your father's house will perish. Yet who knows whether you have come to the kingdom for such a time as this" (Esther 4:14)

We become God's VOICE on the earth for breakthrough by "Praying" His will as we listen and obey.

- He wants us to be His mouthpiece on the earth.
- We can accomplish great things as His mouthpiece.

Heaven responds to our prayers -- God listens and acts on our behalf -- good things happen in the spirit realm when we learn the secret of "**When**" you Pray **"SAY,"**

The Atmosphere changes -- We change -- Our life changes.

Think of what Jeremiah accomplished after he became God's mouthpiece. He was called to "*uproot and tear down, to destroy and overthrow, to build and to plant*" (Jeremiah 1:9-10, NIV).

That's a powerful calling.

Through our prayers, we can do the same. We need the Lord to touch our lips and put His Words in our mouth.

From the beginning of the Bible to its conclusion, we see unequivocal evidence that God answers and responds to The *VOICE* Of Prayer. **Things that we think are impossible; God does when people lift their VOICES and pray.**

*The **VOICE Of Prayer** has won victories over fire, air, earth, and water.*

*The **VOICE Of Prayer** opened the Red Sea.*

*The **VOICE Of Prayer** brought water from the rock and bread from heaven.*

*The **VOICE Of Prayer** made the sun standstill.*

*The **VOICE Of Prayer** brought fire from the sky on Elijah's sacrifice.*

*The **VOICE Of Prayer** overthrew armies and healed the sick.*

*The **VOICE Of Prayer** raised the dead.*

*The **VOICE Of Prayer** has paved the way for the conversion of millions of people.*

When we lift our **VOICES** in Prayer, we align ourselves with the purposes of God and tap into the power of the Almighty. Because we pray, God works through us in ways that He wouldn't otherwise.

God has made certain things dependent upon the **VOICE Of Prayer.** Some things will never be done unless we pray. **Could God do whatever He chooses without our prayer?** Of course! But God has determined that He will use the **VOICE Of the Prayers** of His people to accomplish His purposes on this earth. Therefore, when we do not pray, we limit what God might do in our lives.

Some may not like the sound of this, but if it were not true, what could James mean when he writes, "The Devil is speaking great words against the Most High."?

Daniel 7:24-25, "And the ten horns out of this kingdom are ten kings that shall arise: and another shall rise after them; and he shall be diverse from the first, and he shall subdue three kings." And he shall speak great words against the Most High, and shall wear out the saints of the Most High, and think to change times and laws: and they shall be given into his hand until a time and times and the dividing of time."

PRAYER: *Father, In Jesus' name, today, I receive the grace to be Your Voice of prayer. When I pray, I will Say, Speak, Decree, and Declare by the Power of the Holy Spirit. As I Say in prayer, that atmospheres will change, and we will change -- our life changes forever. Amen!*

CHAPTER 7

WHEN THEY PRAYED

*Several instances are evidencing that "**When**" prayer precedes, things happen. I would like to highlight a few.*

WHEN THEY HAD PRAYED, THE PLACE WAS SHAKEN.

*"And **WHEN they HAD Prayed**, the place was shaken where they were assembled together; and they were all filled with the Holy Ghost, and they spake the word of God with boldness" (Acts 4:31 KJV).*

This remarkable manifestation of God reveals the effectiveness of prayer. It vividly discloses the fact that prayer can accomplish much.

Prayer, Presence, and Purpose.

WHEN THEY HAD PRAYED, THE PLACE...

Places can be defined as our space, our atmosphere, our designated area of life, our sphere of influence, our orbit, our special place as defined by our activity and purposes.

PERSONAL PLACES ARE SHAKEN WHEN WE PRAY.

When Paul and Silas prayed and sang praises; *"Suddenly there was a great earthquake, so that the foundations of the prison were "Shaken" and immediately all the doors were opened and everyone's chains were loosed" (Acts 16:26).*

THE EARTHQUAKE PLACE

Earthquake: The shaking of the surface of the earth caused by underground movement. An earthquake can result in either the raising or lowering of the affected ground.

God can disrupt and shake the deep places in our hearts and lives and rearrange our lives – lifting the parts of our souls that are cast down and bringing low the fragments that are raised in pride, preparing us for God to be seen in our lives.

The earthquake caused

- *The doors to open*
- *The prison to be shaken*
- *The chains to be loosed*

The earthquake is God's hand at work in the deep and invisible places. His working produces lives that are shaken out of captivity and into freedom.

THE PRISON PLACE

Prison: A place of confinement, restriction, punishment, and captivity.

The foundations of the prison shook, not just the walls, but the very underlying support structure. God doesn't merely shake loose a little bit of mortar from the walls that hem you in; He reaches down to the very foundations and upturns them.

> *"Tell them the Lord looked down from his heavenly sanctuary. He looked down to earth from heaven to hear the groans of the prisoners, to release those condemned to die" (Psalm 102:19-20, NLT).*

THE OPENING OF DOORS PLACE

> *"And when they were come, and had gathered the church together, they rehearsed all that God had done with them, and how he had opened the door of faith unto the Gentiles."* (emphasis added, Acts 14:27).

Open: This Greek word "***open***" can merely mean to open a door, but it is also used with other nouns: heavens, eyes, hearing.

While in Acts 16:26, it refers to the opening of the literal prison door, it can also be seen as God opening doors of opportunity, doors of understanding in our hearts, doors of hearing the word of the Lord, and doors of possibility where things were thought impossible.

THE CHAINS LOOSED PLACE

> *"I am the LORD your God, which brought you forth out of the land of Egypt, that ye should not be their bondmen; and I have broken the bands of your yoke, and made you go upright"* (Leviticus 26: 13).

Chains: Anything that binds or ties up someone. In the Old Testament, chains often indicated slavery, not just prison.

When you pray, God will shake you free from every habit, addiction, the secret sin that enslaves you. Amen! Words have power, and God's Word is, above all words. We must pray and speak God's Words over our lives, our homes, our businesses, our church, and our circumstances. Our eye-gate, our ear-gate, and our mouth-gate are all entrances of faith and must be used by the

Holy Spirit to orchestrate His will.

THEY SPOKE THE WORD OF GOD WITH BOLDNESS

Spirit-driven praying consists of a mouth filled with bold declarations from the Word of God, infused with words of power, faith, healing, and blessing.

Pray the Word: Pray the words of God with faith.

Meditate: Think about and rehearse it over and over again.

Declaration: *"I have been moved by the power of God to shake off unwanted things, to break through obstacles, to rise by faith and invade the impossible, and to open my mouth to declare faith declarations boldly." In Jesus' name, Amen!*

Pray Scriptures: *"The Word is near you, in your mouth and in your heart" (that is, the word of faith which we preach): that if you confess with your mouth the Lord Jesus and believe in your heart that God has raised Him from the dead, you will be saved. For with the heart one believes unto righteousness, and with the mouth confession is made unto salvation"* (emphasis added, *Romans 10:8-10).*

> *"Let the words of my mouth and the meditation of my heart Be acceptable in Your sight, O LORD, my strength and my Redeemer"*

(Psalm 19:14, NKJV).

Guard your Heart: The heart is the source, the origin, the point from which flows the life of God. As such, we must exercise great care over what we let enter our hearts. Like the military guard, a city, we must set up guard posts and diligently, with great discipline, guard our hearts. What is in your heart? Fear or faith? The Word of God or the mindset of the world?

> *"Keep your heart with all diligence, for out of it spring the issues of life" (Proverbs 4:23, NKJV).*

> *"Keep vigilant watch over your heart; that's where life starts" (Proverbs 4:23, MSG).*

GUARD YOUR MOUTH:

> *"You are snared by the words of your mouth; You are taken by the words of your mouth" (Proverbs 6:2, NKJV).*

Do not trap yourself by your own words. Whatever you do, don't say what will snare you.

> *"For my mouth will speak truth; Wickedness is an abomination to my lips" (Proverbs 8:7).*
> *"Set a guard, O LORD, over my mouth; Keep watch over the door of my lips" (Psalm 141:3).*

"He who guards his mouth preserves his life, but he who opens wide his lips shall have destruction" (Proverbs 13:3, NKJV).

"Whoever guards his mouth and tongue keeps his soul from trouble" (Proverbs 21:23).

PRAY FAITH-FILLED, WORD FILLED PRAYERS

"Let the word of Christ dwell in you richly in all wisdom, teaching and admonishing one another in psalms and hymns and spiritual songs, singing with grace in your hearts to the Lord" (Colossians 3:16).

"And since we have the same spirit of faith, according to what is written, "I believed and therefore I spoke," we also believe and therefore speak" (2 Corinthians 4:13).

"We're not keeping this quiet, not on your life. Just like the psalmist who wrote, "I believed it, so I said it," we say what we believe" (2 Corinthians 4:13, MSG).

"The scripture says, "I spoke because I believed." In the same spirit of faith, we also speak because we believe" (2 Corinthians 4:13, GNT).

The spirit of faith is the Holy Spirit moving on our spirit. We have a new attitude or outlook of faith.

We declare the absolute greatness and faithfulness of God. We put it in our hearts. We fill our mouths. It is on our lips. It is in us. The word of God is our bread, our life, and our strength. It is true, supernatural, and faithful.

WHEN YOU PRAY, SAY!

We speak/say our prayers with a spirit of faith, a bold spirit of believing and say what we believe, standing on the words we speak. Nothing closes the believer's mouth like unbelief!

"Let the redeemed of the Lord say so, whom He has redeemed from the hand of the enemy (Let those delivered by the Lord speak out, shout out, open your mouth and say it)" (Psalm 107:2).

"For the word of God is living and active. Sharper than any double-edged sword, it penetrates even to dividing soul and spirit, joints and marrow; it judges the thoughts and attitudes of the heart" (Hebrews 4:12, NIV).

THEY SPOKE THE WORD WITH BOLDNESS!

"God means what He says. What he says goes.

His powerful Word is sharp as a surgeon's scalpel, cutting through everything, whether doubt or defense, laying us open to listen and obey" (Hebrews 4:12, MSG).

The Word of God is living and breathing, powerful with the energy of God. It is active and working. When we speak this word, we speak living words, words that have spirit-filled power, breaking power, creative power, fighting the enemy power. When Jesus battled with the devil, He used "*it is* written" as His weapon.

And I SAY, "You are my God."

"But as for me, I trust in You, O LORD; I say, You are my God" (Psalm 31:14).

When you focus on God, not on your problems, God grows greater, and your problems become smaller.

And I SAY continually, "The Lord be magnified."

"Let them shout for joy and be glad, who favor my righteous cause; and let them say continually, "Let the Lord be magnified, who has pleasure in the prosperity of His servant" (Psalm 35:27).

PRAISE HIM CONTINUALLY.

And I SAY, "How awesome are Your works."

"SAY to God, "How awesome are Your works! Through the greatness of Your power Your enemies shall submit themselves to You" (Psalm 66:3).

FOCUS ON HIS AWESOME WORKS.

And I SAY, "You are my refuge and my fortress."

"I will say of the LORD, "He is my refuge and my fortress; My God, in Him I will trust" (Psalm 91:2).

PUT YOUR TRUST IN GOD.

And I SAY, "Your mercy endures forever."

"Let Israel now say, "His mercy endures forever" (Psalm 118:2).

FOCUS ON HIS NEVER-ENDING MERCY.

And I SAY, "You have spoken, and You have fulfilled."

"You have kept what You promised Your servant David my father; You have both spoken with Your mouth and fulfilled it with Your hand, as it is this day" (1 Kings 8:24).

HE WILL DO WHAT HE SAYS!

And I SAY, "Your kingdom come, and Your will be

done."

"Your kingdom come. Your will be done On earth as it is in heaven" (Matthew 6:10).

THE WILL OF THE LORD BE DONE.

And I SAY, "The Lord is on my side. I will not fear."

"The LORD is on my side; I will not fear. What can man do to me?" (Psalm 118:6).

THE ALL-POWERFUL GOD IS ON OUR SIDE.

And I SAY, "He Lord is my confidence. I will not slip."

"For the LORD will be your confidence, and will keep your foot from being caught" (Proverbs 3:26).

THE LORD WILL KEEP YOU FROM FALLING.

And I SAY, "Those who seek the Lord will not lack any good thing."

"The young lions lack and suffer hunger; but those who seek the Lord shall not lack any good thing" (Psalm 34:10).
Let the weak SAY, I am strong (Joel 3:10)
Let the poor SAY, I am rich (Joel 3:10)
Let the sick SAY, with His stripes I am healed

(Isaiah 53:5)

Let the defeated SAY, I am more than a conqueror in Christ Jesus (Romans 8:37)

Let the redeemed of the Lord SAY so. (Psalms 107:2)

THE RIGHTEOUS HAVE NEVER BEEN FORSAKEN.

WHEN you **PRAY**, **SAY,** and you will have what you **SAY**! Amen!

CHAPTER 8

WHEN SOLOMON FINISHED PRAYING FIRE AND GLORY

*"When Solomon finished praying, **FIRE** came down from heaven and consumed the burnt offering and the sacrifices, and the GLORY of the LORD filled the temple" (2 Chronicles 7:1 NIV).*

Solomon's prayer started in chapter six;

*"And he stood before the altar of the LORD in the presence of all the congregation of Israel, and spread forth his hands: For Solomon had made a brazen scaffold, of five cubits long, and five cubits broad, and three cubits high, and had set it in the midst of the court: **and upon it he stood, and kneeled down upon his knees before all the congregation of Israel, and spread forth his hands toward heaven, And said,** O LORD God of Israel, there is no God like thee in the*

heaven, nor in the earth; which keepest covenant, and showest mercy unto thy servants, that walk before thee with all their hearts" (2 Chronicles 6:12-14).

Four things are evident as Solomon prayed:

1. He stood
2. He Kneeled
3. He spread his hands towards heaven.
4. And he Said

When you pray, "**SAY**."

Three out of the four are called Prayer Postures, which I will present later. Prayer Postures are just as important as what we SAY in prayer, and scripture finds them noteworthy hence, they are mentioned. Again, we see the principle of "When" and not "If" we pray that releases a response from heaven.

IT WAS A PRAYER OF DEDICATION:

Now they were to have a permanent place of worship and witness, a place of fixity, solidity, and beauty. It was here that the divine Presence was manifested.

This day of dedication was a long-awaited day. The Temple had been seven years in building (I Kings 6:38), and now a vast crowd assembled for the history-making occasion. The King himself prayed the dedicatory prayer recorded here in 2 Chronicles 6.

THE BEGINNING OF SOLOMON'S PRAYER

"Then Solomon stood before the altar of the LORD in the presence of all the assembly of Israel, for Solomon had made a brazen scaffold, of five cubits long, and five cubits broad, and three cubits high, and had set it in the midst of the court: and upon, it he stood, and kneeled down upon his knees before the congregation of Israel, and spread forth his hands toward heaven, And said, "LORD God of Israel, there is no God in heaven above or on earth below like You, who keep Your covenant and mercy with Your servants who walk before You with all their hearts."

Here we note -

SOLOMON'S PRAYER PLACE:

"Then Solomon stood before the Altar of the LORD in the presence of all the assembly of Israel..." This was a public prayer. He prays best in public who prays most in private.

SOLOMON'S PRAYER POSTURE'S:

He Stood

"When you Stand praying" (Mark 11:24).

He Knelt

"For this cause I bow my knees unto the Father
of our Lord Jesus Christ" (Ephesians 3:14).

Frequent kneeling keeps us in good standing with God!
He both knelt and stood.

He spread forth his hands toward heaven

"Let us lift up our heart with our hands unto
God in the heavens" (Lamentations 3:41).

This is a posture of reverence, resignation, dependence, and reliance. When we come before God in this attitude, we are saying by our posture, "Here I am, totally surrendered and subservient to Your sovereignty and dependent upon Your mercy, O God! We are to come boldly to the Throne but humbly as well.

When Solomon had finished praying all this prayer and supplication to the LORD, that he arose from before the altar of the LORD, from kneeling on his knees with his hands spread up to heaven."
He both knelt and stood.

There is no one posture for which we should regard greater than the other; It is the posture of the heart that matters most with God.

He predicated his prayer upon the promises of God.

"For all the promises of God in him are yea, and in him Amen, unto the glory of God by us" (2 Corinthians 1:20).

He referred to the promises that God made about the Temple. God is a promise maker and a promise keeper. "When" you pray, refer to the promises of God concerning you and your future. The promises that God made to David were being fulfilled at the very moment Solomon was speaking. The Temple had been built and was now being dedicated.

He reminds God about the promise made about the Throne.

"Therefore, LORD God of Israel, now keep what You promised Your servant David my father, saying, 'You shall not fail to have a man sit before Me on the throne of Israel, only if your sons take heed to their way, that they walk before Me as you have walked before Me.' And now I pray, O God of Israel, let Your Word come true, which You have spoken to Your servant David my father" (1 Kings 8: 25, 26).

He is looking to the future of the nation; he has perpetuity in mind. Unless God's man is on the throne and by him, the nation is preserved and perpetuated, with God's blessings, the Temple will be destroyed.

I DECREE *that God will establish His Kingship and Kingdom in your temple that it will never be destroyed in Jesus' name.*

Praying the promises of God is the Bible's way of praying. Solomon, when praying, cites the promises of God, claims the promises, and clings to them. The lesson for us? Get a promise in God's Word and run to the throne of God with it if you want to gain God's ear!

PROMISES TO STAND ON

- Provision for our needs (Matthew 6:25-34).
- Answer to prayer (Matthew 7:7-11; 1 John 5:14,15).
- All we need to live for Him (2 Peter 1:3, 4).
- Rewards for service (2 Corinthians 5:10).
- Help in our praying (Romans 8:26).
- Eternal life (John 3:16; 5:24).
- A home in heaven (John 14:1-4).
- Assurance of salvation (John 10:29).
- The Holy Spirit within (Ephesians 1:13, 14).
- Spiritual gifts (Romans 12:3-8; 1 Cor. 12).
- Forgiveness for daily sins (1 John 1:9).

- Peace of mind (Philippians 4:7).
- A way to defeat temptation (1 Corinthians 10:13).
- Wisdom in times of testing (James 1:5).
- Power for living (Ephesians 1:19; 3:20).
- Access to God through prayer (Ephesians 3:12).
- Mercy and grace in times of need (Hebrews 4:16).
- The illumination of the Spirit (1 Corinthians 2:6-16).
- Freedom from sin's grip (Romans 6:22).
- Loving discipline (Hebrews 12:3-11).
- Ability to make Satan flee (James 4:7).
- Resurrection to glory (1 Thessalonians 4:16, 17).
- Strength to do God's will (Philippians 4:13).

There are 365 promises in the Bible, one for each day of the year.

GOD ANSWERED WITH FIRE AND GLORY:

"When Solomon finished praying, FIRE came down from heaven and consumed the burnt offering and the sacrifices, and the GLORY of the LORD filled the temple" (2 Chronicles 7:1, NIV).

"Therefore understand today that the LORD Your God is He who goes over before you as a

consuming fire. He will destroy them and bring them down before you; so you shall drive them out and destroy them quickly, as the LORD has said to you." (Deuteronomy 9:3)

"The sight of the glory of the LORD was like a consuming fire on the top of the mountain in the eyes of the children of Israel" (Exodus 24:17).

*"For the LORD your God **IS A consuming fire,** a jealous God" (Deuteronomy 4:24).*

Here we see that the LORD your God is not just as a consuming fire or was like a consuming fire but IS A CONSUMING FIRE. It is one of His attributes.

Consume - (Webster's 1828 Dictionary)

- To destroy, by separating the parts of a thing, by decomposition, as by fire, or eating, devouring, and annihilating the form of a substance.
- Fire consumes wood, coal, stubble; animals consume flesh and vegetables.
- **It also means to eat completely or entirely: to devour.**

The term *Fire of God* is often used symbolically in the Bible to portray the presence of God, the power of God, His judgment, His purifying work, and, as His emblem of the anointing. Fire is often the Manifestation of God Himself. Fire is a strange and fearful weapon. No power can come against the *Fire of God* and not get burned to ashes.

SOME MAJOR EFFECTS OF FIRE:

It gives warmth: We sit in front of a fire to be warmed, encouraged, and cheered up.

FIRE illuminates: Fire sends out an illuminating ray, fire sheds forth light.

FIRE preserves: people are looking for preservation.

FIRE purifies and refines: Diamond, gold, and silver are always being refined and purify by fire.

FIRE fuses: Mix a heap of iron ore with some earth. How can the metal be separated from the earth to become a glowing mass? Well, the ore must be flung into a white-hot furnace and the fire fanned by a powerful draught so that it plays upon the mass of ore and earth until the dross separates from the metal, and the metal is then fused into a molten mass.

FIRE energizes: If fire is put into a steam engine, great energy is generated.

FIRE burns: Fire will burn any combustible matter it

encounters! All one has to do is see the devastation of a house fire, and the point is obvious.

Satan doesn't easily cross the region of fire; if you are on fire, the devil cannot touch you.

> *"Who maketh His angels spirits; His ministers a flaming fire" (Psalm 104:4).*

FIRE destroys and keeps away wild beasts.

FIRE has penetrating power.

FIRE is aggressive and militant.

The light of ***FIRE offers direction***.

FIRE speaks.

FIRE is hot and makes no compromise.

FIRE is very confrontational.

FIRE has dominion power.

FIRE does not respect any law

FIRE does not fit into solid or liquid,

FIRE does not obey the law of matter or gravitation.

FIRE melts down and separates.

FIRE is focused.

FIRE has no respect; when you throw fire into the forest, it does not discriminate between the elephant and the ant; it consumes all. When there is a fire outbreak in the forest, all the animals will run and scatter.

FIRE is destructive and powerful. Spiritually, it can warn us of impending danger ahead.

However, the advantage of ***FIRE*** is a factor of an early warning, which would create a sign of safety. So, the Bible describing God as "a consuming fire", is not surprising that fire often appears as a symbol of God's presence.

Therefore, the context of "When Solomon had finished praying ***FIRE*** *came down from heaven and CONSUMED the burnt offering and the sacrifices, and the GLORY of the LORD filled the temple" (2 Chronicles 7:1, NIV)* means the fire was the Manifestation of the Presence of God in response or as an answer to the Prayer of Solomon.

The LORD was pleased with the Prayer. The sign of approval was The Fire fell not only to consume the wood, coal, stubble, flesh of animal sacrifices placed on the Altar, but it also meant to eat (consume) completely or entirely: to devour.

The LORD, who is A CONSUMING FIRE,

CONSUMED the sacrifice in acceptance of the Prayers offered by Solomon.

Secondly, the GLORY of the LORD filled the temple. If the scripture categorically states, the GLORY of the LORD, it means there were other glories that had occupied the temple that had drawn man's attention to himself as opposed to God, as in glorying in his own wisdom, might, and riches which caused the Glory of God to depart.

The Glory Is one of the mystical concepts of God, which I prefer to discuss in detail perhaps at another time to give it its due merit within human understanding. The glory of God isn't just a feeling, an event, or an Old Testament experience; it's a spiritual encompassing of everything contained in the character of God.

- The Glory of God is elusive; it's difficult to describe, detect, or grasp by the mind.
- The Glory of God is an abstract concept; its elusive, indefinable, and not easily profiled.
- The Glory of God belongs to the mystical concepts of God.
- The Glory can't be preached, taught, articulated, or explained.
- The Glory of God cannot be known academically

–

- The Glory of God cannot be known intellectually; it's not a theory or doctrine or philosophy or an ideology.
- The Glory of God is hard to comprehend.
- The Glory of God is an Epiphany which is a divine manifestation of God.
- The Glory of God has to be discerned, perceived, and experienced.
- The Glory of God is the visible, tangible manifestation of the invisible God.
- The Glory of God is what brings us into the reality of the true and living God; It's an experience as a result of the manifested Presence of God in a place.

We, as the people of God, must have an acquaintance or be acquainted with the glory. It's possible to be in a glory zone and yet be unaware of his presence.

There are 2 Greek words used for glory in the Bible:

1. Doxa – Doxology – To honor, to esteem highly, and express to have a favorable opinion about God speaking of Him as being the source from whom all divine splendor and perfection precede in their manifestation. Doxa – glory; The honor,

praise, and glory that comes from a seen manifestation. It's an appearance commanding respect, excellence, and magnificence. This term is used to describe God's nature and actions in self-manifestation. It's who He is and is shown through what He does, especially in how He chooses to reveal Himself to us.

"And the Word became flesh and dwelt among us, and we beheld His glory, the glory as of the only begotten of the Father, full of grace and truth" (John 1:14).

Scripture declares;

"Thus saith the LORD, Let not the wise man glory in his wisdom, neither let the mighty man glory in his might, let not the rich man glory in his riches. But let him that glorieth glory in this, that he understandeth and knoweth me, that I am the LORD which exercise lovingkindness, judgment, and righteousness, in the earth: for in these things I delight, saith the LORD" (Jeremiah 9:23-24).

"I am the LORD: that is my name: and my glory will I not give to another, neither my

praise to graven images" (Isaiah 42:8).

Glory is His Kingdom, and He is the King of Glory. So, God guards His both Glory jealousy.

"Lift up your heads, O ye gates; and be ye lift up, ye everlasting doors; and the King of glory shall come in. Who is this King of glory? The LORD strong and mighty, the LORD mighty in battle. Lift up your heads, O ye gates; even lift them up, ye everlasting doors; and the King of glory shall come in. Who is this King of glory? **The LORD of hosts, He is the King of glory.** *Selah" (Psalm 24:7-10).*

WHEN THE FIRE AND GLORY CAME:

a. Everyone fell to their knees on the pavement (hard place) and worshiped and praised God. Solomon the King was the example; leadership must live by example.

b. The Priests could not enter or minister because of the Glory.

c. The King and all the people offered sacrifices before the LORD. No one pushed or pleaded with people to give; they gave willingly.

"And the LORD appeared to Solomon by night, and said unto him, **I have heard thy prayer,** *and*

have chosen this place to myself for a house of sacrifice. If I shut up heaven that there be no rain, or if I command the locusts to devour the land, or if I send pestilence among my people; If my people, which are called by my name, shall humble themselves, and pray, and seek my face, and turn from their wicked ways; then will I hear from heaven, and will forgive their sin, and will heal their land. Now mine eyes shall be open, and mine ears attentive unto the prayer that is made in this place. For now have I chosen and sanctified this house that my name may be there forever: and mine eyes and mine heart shall be there perpetually. And as for thee, if thou wilt walk before me, as David thy father walked, and do according to all that I have commanded thee, and shalt observe my statutes and my judgments; Then will I stablish the throne of thy kingdom, according as I have covenanted with David thy father, saying, There shall not fail thee a man to be ruler in Israel"
(2 Chronicles 7:12-18).

MAY THE LORD HEAR AND ANSWER YOU WITH FIRE AND HIS GLORY WHEN YOU PRAY.

CHAPTER 9

Promises Concerning Answers
To Prayer

God gives amazing promises concerning His heart to answer the prayers of His people. Some of these promises have conditions, and some do not.
Notice the following verses:

> *"If My people who are called by My name will humble themselves, and pray and seek My face, and turn from their wicked ways, then I will hear from heaven, and will forgive their sin and heal their land" (II Chronicles 7:14).*

> *"The eyes of the LORD are on the righteous, and His ears are open to their cry" (Psalm 34:1).*

> *"Delight yourself also in the LORD, and He shall give you the desires of your heart. Commit your way to the LORD, trust also in Him, and He shall bring it to pass" (Psalm 37:4-5).*

"Because he has set his love upon Me, therefore I will deliver him; I will set him on high, because he has known My name. He shall call upon Me, and I will answer him; I will be with him in trouble; I will deliver him and honor him" (Psalm 91:14-15).

"Ask, and it will be given to you; seek, and you will find; knock, and it will be opened to you. For everyone who asks receives, and he who seeks finds, and to him who knocks it will be opened. Or what man is there among you who, if his son asks for bread, will give him a stone? Or if he asks for a fish, will he give him a serpent? If you then, being evil, know how to give good gifts to your children, how much more will your Father who is in heaven give good things to those who ask Him (Matthew 7:7-11).

"Again I say to you that if two of you agree on earth concerning anything that they ask, it will be done for them by My Father in heaven. For where two or three are gathered together in My name, I am there in the midst of them" (Matthew 18:19-20).

"For assuredly, I say to you, whoever says to this mountain, "Be removed and be cast into the sea," and does not doubt in his heart, but believes that those things he says will be done, he will have whatever he says. Therefore I say to you, whatever things you ask when you pray, believe that you receive them, and you will have them" (Mark 11:23-24).

"Most assuredly, I say to you, he who believes in Me, the works that I do he will do also; and greater works than these he will do, because I go to My Father. And whatever you ask in My name, that I will do, that the Father may be glorified in the Son. If you ask anything in My name, I will do it" (John 14:12-14).

"If you abide in Me, and My words abide in you, you will ask what you desire, and it shall be done for you" (John 15:7).

"And in that day you will ask Me nothing. Most assuredly, I say to you, whatever you ask the Father in My name He will give you. Until now you have asked nothing in My name. Ask, and you will receive, that your joy may be full"

(John 16:23-24).

"If any of you lacks wisdom, let him ask of God, who gives to all liberally and without reproach, and it will be given to him. But let him ask in faith, with no doubting, for he who doubts is like a wave of the sea driven and tossed by the wind. For let not that man suppose that he will receive anything from the Lord; he is a double-minded man, unstable in all his ways" (James 1:5-8).

"And whatever we ask we receive from Him, because we keep His commandments and do those things that are pleasing in His sight. And this is His commandment: that we should believe on the name of His Son Jesus Christ and love one another, as He gave us commandment" (I John 3:22).

"Now this is the confidence that we have in Him, that if we ask anything according to His will, He hears us. And if we know that He hears us, whatever we ask, we know that we have the petitions that we have asked of Him" (I John 5:14-15).

Notice some of the things that these verses tell us

about God's desire to answer prayer.

1. God wants to answer our prayer.
2. God wants us to be fruitful.
3. God wants us to be successful.
4. God only wants good for us.

Notice some of the conditions for answered prayer in many of the verses. We increase our potential for answered prayer when...

1. We walk humbly before the Lord (I Chronicles 7:14).
2. We are honest in dealing with the sin issues in our lives (Isaiah 59:1-2).
3. We seek His face (I Chronicles 7:14).
4. We keep His commandments (I John 3:22).
5. We walk in love (I John 3:22).
6. We abide in Him (John 15:7).
7. We delight ourselves in Him (Psalms 37:4).
8. We have faith in His desire and ability to do what we ask (James 1:5-8).
9. We ask in Jesus' name (John 16:23-24).
10. We ask according to His will (I John 5:14-15).

Here Are Some Scripture References to Jump Start your WHEN You PRAY:

PRAYER

- Isaiah 65:24 ...before they call, I will answer...
- Psalm 37:4...delight in the Lord, he gives desires of your heart...
- Psalm 37:5...commit your way to Lord; He will bring it to pass...
- Jeremiah 33:3 ...call on me, and I will show you great, and mighty things
- Jeremiah 32:17-18 ...you have made heaven...nothing is too hard for you...
- Matthew 18:19 ...if any 2 agree...touch...ask, it will be done...

PEACE

- Isaiah 26:3...keep you in perfect peace...
- Isaiah 32:17 ...work of righteousness will be peace...
- Jeremiah 29:11 ...the thoughts I think toward you are peace, not evil... Psalm 37:37 ...the end of the upright man is peace...

PROTECTION

- Psalm 91:3...he shall deliver from snare, pestilence, terror, arrow...
- Isaiah 54:17 ...no weapon formed against you will prosper... Isaiah 43:2

- ...when you pass through water, it will not overflow you...
- Jeremiah 15:20 ...I will make you a steel wall; they will not prevail... Psalm 5:11-12 ...those who trust you, shout for joy, you defend them...

SUPPLY

- Psalm 34:10...lions do hunger...but you shall not lack any good thing... Psalm 37:25...I have not seen the righteous forsaken or begging...
- Philippians 4:19 ...my God shall supply all your need...
- II Corinthians 9:8 ...God is able to make all grace abound to you...

SUCCESS

- Joshua 1:8 ...then you shall make way prosperous, and have success Psalm 1:3 ...whatsoever he does it shall prosper...
- Romans 8:28 ...all things work together for good to him...

STRENGTH

- Isaiah 40:29 ...He gives power to the faint...
- Isaiah 40:31 ...they that wait on the Lord renew their strength... Isaiah 41:10
- ...fear not for I am with you...I will help you

Isaiah 41:13 ...the Lord will hold your right hand...

- II Corinthians 12:9 ...my grace is sufficient for you...

DELIVERANCE

- Psalm 34:17,19 ...the righteous cry and the Lord hears and delivers from trouble Psalm 34:7,8 ...angel encamps around those who fear Him...
- Isaiah 59:19 ...when the enemy comes like a flood, the Lord will stand against him.

DIRECTION AND LEADING

- Proverbs 3:6 ...In all your ways acknowledge Him, and He will direct your paths...
- Isaiah 30:21 ...you will hear a word behind you saying, "this is the way, walk in it."
- Proverbs 16:3,9 ...commit your way to the Lord ...and your thoughts will be established...
- Psalm 37:23 ...a good man's steps are ordered by the Lord.
- Isaiah 58:11 ...the Lord will guide you continually...
- Psalm 32:8...I will instruct & teach you the way to go...

FEARS

- II Timothy 1:7 ...God did not give the spirit of fear, but a sound mind...
- Isaiah 41:10 ...fear not for I am with you; I will help you...
- Isaiah 41:13...fear not I will help you...

SOULS

- Psalm 2:8 ...ask of Me, and I will give heathen for your inheritance... Psalm 126:6 ...he who sows and weeps...shall bring sheaves with him...
- II Peter 3:9 ...Lord is not slack...not willing any should perish...

YOUR CHILDREN

- Isaiah 54:11-13 ...all your children will be taught of the Lord...
- Psalm 127:3 ...children are a heritage of the Lord...your reward...
- Isaiah 59:21 ...my words will not depart out of your seed's mouth...
- Isaiah 44:3 ...I will pour out my Spirit on your seed and offspring...
- Proverbs 22:6 ...train up a child...when old...he will not depart from it...

WISDOM

- Isaiah 50:4 ...Lord gives me the tongue of the

learned to know how to speak...

- Psalm 19:7 ...The law...is perfect...making wise the simple...
- Proverbs 1:7 ...Fear of the Lord is the beginning of knowledge...
- James 1:5 ...lack wisdom? Ask of God that gives liberally to all men...

FORGIVENESS

- Psalm 86:5 ...thou Lord art good...ready to forgive...
- I John 1:9 ...If we confess our sins, He is faithful...to forgive...all...
- Isaiah 1:18 ...though your sins be as scarlet they shall be white as snow
- Isaiah 43:25 ...I am He that blots out transgressions...

ABILITY ABOVE IMPOSSIBILITY

- Jeremiah 32:17, 27... The Lord God... there is nothing too hard for You...
- Philippians 1:6 ...he that began a good work in you will perform it...
- Acts 20:32 ...the word of His grace... is able to build you up...
- Ephesians 3:20 ...able to exceedingly

abundantly...by the power in us...

- Jude 24 ...able to keep you...present you faultless...

HEALING

- Exodus 15:26 ...I Am the Lord that healeth thee
- Psalm 103:3-4 ...who forgiveth all...healeth all thy diseases...
- James 5:15 ...the prayer of faith shall save the sick...
- Matthew 8:17 ...He took our infirmities and carried our diseases...

SLEEP

- Proverbs 3:24 ...you shall lie down, and your sleep will be sweet...
- Psalm 4:8 ...I will...sleep, for you make me dwell in safety...
- Psalm 127:2 ...for so He gives His beloved sleep...

WORD OF GOD

- Isaiah 55:11 ...shall not return void...shall accomplish and prosper...
- Jeremiah 23:29 ...Is not my word like a fire...like a hammer

- Acts 20:32 ...which is able to build you up and give you an inheritance
- Hebrews 4:12 ...is quick, powerful, sharp, piercing, dividing, discerning...
- 2 Timothy 2:9 ...word of God is not bound...
- 2 Timothy 3:16 ...is profitable for doctrine, reproof, instruction...

FINAL THOUGHTS WHEN YOU PRAY

GET INTO THE HABIT OF PRAYER.

a. Set aside time. Take time when it can best be found, preferably early in the day. Prayers that are not said in the morning tend not to be said at all.

b. Set a minimum time. Begin modestly but gradually increase in length. Ten minutes is a realistic minimum, and a half-hour is within most people's ability. Stretch to at least one hour.

c. Be faithful. Whatever length of time is decided, it should be firmly kept. Without some discipline, prayer tends to be pushed to the margin even by the most devout - there is always something else to do that appears more pressing or more attractive. There are days when prayer seems less natural and spontaneous, and concentration is harder. On these days, the offering of time is an act of obedience - which is itself an act of faith.

d.   Have structure. Having structure can give shape on constancy without constricting your spontaneous approach to God.

Begin with acknowledging the presence of God. Adoration follows praise, awe, and love for who He is. Then, follow where the personal situation leads.

Personal situations may include thanks for particular benefits or mercies to you and others, admission of sins, and requests for your desires or needs, intercession for the help of others. Don't worry if one area monopolizes your prayer time - consider this as a principal need of the day.

e.   Ask. Prayer is not a shopping list of things you'd like to have, yet it is right to bring your hopes before God, and in so doing, to test their quality. But you are encouraged and even commanded to ask so that your relationship with Him includes all aspects of your life. As you make intercession for others, ask that you be made available to be used in God's service if the opportunity is given.

f.   Be ambitious, but not impatient. All Christians, including the saints, have known periods when there seems to be no progress. These are times to hold fast to the discipline of prayer, waiting until you are ready to receive God's calling to new understanding and fresh devotion.

g. Use a good prayer book(s). There is strength in praying established prayers in addition to your personal prayers. The insights and phrasing of these prayers can expand your understanding of God and help in articulation of thought and vocabulary. Remember the Lord's Prayer, which gives you a perfect pattern for prayer. Commit to praying it with a renewed awareness of the words. (For additional prayer resources, please visit our online bookstore at:

www.prayeracademyglobalbookstore.org).

h. Prayer is a relationship. Essentially prayer brings you into contact with God. Your growth in prayer should be a deepening of that relationship with Him. Like a child who runs eagerly with requests to a loving parent, your sincerity and complete honesty are essential for prayer as you run to the Father.

PRACTICAL DISCIPLINES:

1. **PRAY FOR YOURSELF:**

a. Your troubles

b. Your aches & pains

c. Your faith & faithfulness

d. Your courage to witness

e. Your heart's secret goals

f. Your needs, provisions

g. Your finances, funds

h. Your enemies

i. Your struggles

j. Your finances

k. Your temptations

l. Your heart secret desires and fears

m. Your courage to witness

2. PRAY FOR YOUR FUTURE:

a. Your plans

b. Your goals

c. Your ministries

d. Your vision

3. PRAY FOR YOUR FAMILY:

a. Each member by name and need

b. Spouse needs

c. Spiritual growth & love of all in family

d. Health and safety

e. Protection from evil & temptation

4. Pray for your faults

  c. Your struggles

  d. Your worries

  e. Salvation of children

The longer I am a Christian, the more I believe in the power of prayer. *Prayer is the Master Key*.

- I **BELIEVE** that God hears and answers us when we speak to Him.

- I **BELIEVE** that God wants us to pray to Him in worship as well as petition.

- I **BELIEVE** that a Christian who does not have a consistent prayer life is missing one of the greatest joys of being a Christian.

- I **BELIEVE** that the Church that takes prayer seriously is a Church that will bring glory to God.

- I **BELIEVE** that anything that is not birthed through prayer is illegal in the earth realm.

"WHEN" YOU PRAY NOT "IF" YOU PRAY!

DAILY DECLARATIONS

You have the authority to decree a thing.

*"Thou shalt also **Decree** a thing, and it shall be established unto thee: and the light shall shine upon thy ways" (Job 22:28).*

Speak these declarations over your life DAILY with expectation:

I DECREE the keys of the kingdom of heaven have been given to me, and whatsoever I bind on earth is bound in heaven, and whatsoever I loose on earth is loosed in heaven (Matthew 16:19).

I DECREE no weapon formed against me shall prosper, and every tongue that shall rise against me in judgment shall be condemned (Isaiah 54:17).

I DECREE I am blessed coming in and blessed going out. I am the head and not the tail, above only, and not beneath (Deuteronomy 28:13).

I DECREE I am strong in the Lord and the power of His might as I put on the whole armor of God and stand against all the wiles of the devil (Ephesians 6:11).

I DECREE my steps are ordered every day by the Lord (Psalm 37:23).

I DECREE all things work together for my good because I love God and are called according to His purpose (Romans 8:28).

I DECREE God is my refuge and strength, a very present help in times of trouble (Psalms 46:1).

I DECREE God has not given me the spirit of fear, but of power, love, and a sound mind (2 Timothy 1:7).

I DECREE the LORD renews my strength; I mount up with wings as eagles; I run, and shall not be weary, walk, and faint not (Isaiah 40:31).

I DECREE the favor of God. If God be for me, who can be against me? (Romans 8:31).

I DECREE I give, and it shall be given back to me; good measure, pressed down, shaken together, and running over, shall men give into my bosom (Luke 6:38).

I DECREE I delight myself in the LORD, and he gives me the desires of my heart (Psalms 37:4).

I DECREE I have the peace of God that passes all understanding (Philippians 4:7).

I DECREE I am a believer with signs follow me. In the Name of Jesus, I cast out devils, speak with new tongues, take up serpents, and if I drink any deadly thing, it will not harm me; I lay hands on the sick, and they recover (Mark 16:17-19).

I DECREE greater is He that lives in me than he that lives in the world (1 John 4:4).

I DECREE My God supplies all of my needs according to His riches in glory by Christ Jesus (Philippians 4:19).

I DECREE by His stripes; I am healed (1 Peter 2:24).

I DECREE I am born of God, and the evil one cannot touch me (1 John 5:18).

I DECREE I call on the Lord, and He answers me and shows me great and mighty things I know not of (Jeremiah 33:3).

I DECREE I have been given the power to tread on serpents and scorpions, and overall the power of the enemy: and nothing shall by any means hurt me. (Luke 10:19)

I DECREE God gives me the treasures of darkness and hidden riches of secret places that I may know that the LORD is God. (Isaiah 45:3)

I DECREE God is not a man that he should lie to me, neither the son of man that he should change His mind. The things he has said, he will do, and the things he has spoken he will make good. (Numbers 23:19)

I DECREE wealth and riches shall be in my house because I fear the Lord. (Psalm 112:3)

I DECREE the kingdom of God come, in my life, family, marriage, ministry, relationships, and work. (Matthew 6:10)

I DECREE I am satisfied with the words of my mouth because life and death are in the power of my tongue. Proverbs 18:20

I DECREE, with absolute faith by God's eternal Spirit of grace and mercy that I now inhabit heavenly places and sit high above all principality and power, might and dominions and every name that is named! Thus, I work, walk, talk, and think in authority and exercise my right to be rich and live the abundant lifestyle given unto me by Christ Jesus, in Jesus' name (Ephesians 1:12-23, 2:4).

I DECREE with absolute faith that today going forward. I operate outside this world's system and accumulate wealth, health, riches, honor, and blessing supernaturally by divine providence, favor, mercy, in Jesus' name!

(Philippians 4:19).

I DECREE with absolute faith that as an heir of God and joint-heir with Christ I have a right to be rich, prosperous and well satisfied in all areas of my life with plenty to give and enough to meet all needs that arise with plenty to spare, in Jesus' name (2 Corinthians 9:6-12)

I DECREE with absolute faith that the divine will of God is for me to dwell in my wealthy place! Multiple channels of prosperity, riches, health, wealth, abundance, and financial increase come into, invade and saturate my life now in Jesus' name! Deuteronomy 28:1-14

I DECREE with absolute faith that my hearing is acute, fine-tuned, bent toward His heart and magnetized to the voice of the Holy Spirit who shall speak to me, lead and guide me into my wealthy place. Thus, I will trust, follow, and execute the plans of the Spirit to achieve my destination and inhabit this fabulous place (Isaiah 48:15-18).

I DECREE with absolute faith that I have arrived in my wealthy place of abundance, prosperity, riches, spiritual power, wisdom, and blessing!

The blessing of Abraham has exploded in my life, and I now have become a channel for God's unlimited flow of supplies and a vessel prepared for His use, n Jesus' name (Psalm 66:12, 2 Peter 1:3-11, Galatians 3:13-14).

I DECREE with absolute faith that God is my source using many channels, of which I am one, to bless His people and accomplish His will in the earth realm.

As a channel, I open myself up to receive and release by faith, healing, empowerment, salvation, wisdom, knowledge, creative ideas, increase, blessing, the anointing, discernment, love, reconciliation, restoration, deliverance, stability, and grace all, in Jesus' name (Isaiah 60).

I DECREE with absolute faith that I let the wisdom of God overshadow my spirit, mind, soul, and body that I may be guided in what to say, how to say it and to whom to say it to, in Jesus' name (Isaiah 55:11-13).

I DECREE with absolute faith that every day I expect, experience, and manifest the miracles of the kingdom, which validate, vindicate, and confirm the Word of God in the earth realm (Psalm 62:5).

I DECREE with absolute faith that I walk, operate, pray, and speak through the Spirit. I see, hear, and manifest the things of the Spirit through the fruit and gifts of the Spirit of God. Through my spiritual connection with the

righteousness, judgment, and

Kingdom of God, I receive, I am entitled to, and embrace the prepared blessings that have been reserved, revealed, transferred and released into my life, family, and church (1 Corinthians 2:9-12).

I DECREE with absolute faith that today forward, I believe all things are possible through the anointing, the Word, and recognizing God as my source (Luke 1:37).

I DECREE with absolute faith that today, my heart is filled with the presence of God and will forever provide a place for His habitation, demonstration, and power! (2 Corinthians 4:7).

I DECREE with absolute faith that I walk under the anointing of Christ, which has destroyed all yokes, links, chains, and strongholds connected to my life and all those I connect with. Setting all completely, free financially, physically, spiritually, and emotionally (Isaiah 10:27, Jonah 8:32,36, 2 Corinthians 10:3-6).

I DECREE with absolute faith that today I flow in the anointing of Christ, the grace of God, and empowerment of the Holy Spirit for the fulfillment of His will for my life and advancement of humanity, family, and the kingdom. (Isaiah 11:1-4, Luke 10:19-20, Acts 1:8).

I DECREE with absolute faith that the spirit of fear, doubt, unbelief, disobedience, and deception are broken and eliminated from my life, family, ministry, and church. Thus, I now flow with the Trinity in peace, power, wisdom, understanding, knowledge, gifts, skills, talents of the Kingdom of God for the manifestation of His Glory in the earth realm (John 7:38-39, 16:13-16).

I DECREE with absolute faith that from this day forward, I'll never be broke again another day of my life. The anointing has destroyed all yokes, chains, hindrances, restrictions, obstacles, and dams that have blocked all forms of increase, prosperity, advancement, elevations, and promotions that were ordained for the fulfillment of God's will in my life, family, and church (Isaiah 10:27, 2 Corinthians 8:9).

I DECREE with absolute faith that the Lord is my shepherd and I shall not want! He restores my soul, anoints my head, mind, and spirit and makes my soul over ow with joy, peace, power, the anointing, love, vision, dreams, directions, favor, and patience (Psalm 23).

I DECREE with absolute faith that I through, the anointing of God shall not want, have, lack, experience poverty or suffer need but shall be completely supplied with all blessings both natural and spiritual to fulfill my destiny! Thus I attract abundance in all forms, experience financial freedom, become a lender, the head above only, and obtain all resources from God my only source, in the form of gifts, donations, rewards, grants, business transactions, miracles, divine manifestations, wealth transfers and the like that I may excel, advance the Kingdom of God and establish His covenant in the earth realm and bring Glory to His name (1 Chronicles 29:11-12, Deuteronomy 28:1-14).

I DECREE with absolute faith that today, supernatural debt cancellation has taken place in my life, ministry, family and church, wealth, riches, prosperity, all currencies, and financial elevation comes into my life now without delay, in Jesus' name (Genesis 12:1-3, 13:1-2).

I DECREE with absolute faith that today, this is my DECADE of DESTINY DELIVERY AND DESTINY FULFILLMENT, IN JESUS' NAME! AMEN!

.

YOUR COVENANT COMMITMENT TO THE MINISTRY

1. PRAY daily for at least 15 minutes.
2. PRAY daily for divine protection for my family and me, as well as for our worldwide ministry team and their families, and our entire ministry.
3. PRAY daily for a harvest of souls around the world.
4. PRAY daily for your nation, its government, your church leaders, and for spiritual revival.
5. PRAY daily for the urgent prayer requests that come to the ministry from God's people around the globe.
6. PRAY daily for the other prayer warriors in this mighty army.
7. PRAISE God daily for the victories He is pouring upon the lives of His people.

OUR COVENANT COMMITMENT TO YOU

1. My team and I promise to pray daily for you and your loved ones.
2. You will be able to submit your prayer requests and praise reports directly to my private e-mail address explicitly reserved for members of the Prayer Academy, Elite Warriors.
3. We will stand in the gap on your behalf until you get the victory.
4. We will send you e-mails for special events that are occurring, as well as urgent prayer requests from people around the globe.

PRAYER DECLARATION SERIES BY SARAH MORGAN

1. Activating and Affirming God's Prophecies and Promises
2. Affirmations of Faith
3. Blessed State of the Righteous
4. Breaking the Anti-Marriage Spirit
5. Breaking Dream Killers
6. Chain Breakers
7. Children's Prayers
8. Cleansing from Defilement
9. Destroying the Spirit of Stagnancy
10. Finances-Prosperity
11. Healing Prayer
12. Healing is for You
13. I Am Declarations
14. Praying by the Blood of Jesus
15. Prayers for Healing
16. Prayer for Husbands
17. Prophetic Call
18. Pursue and Overtake and Recover
19. Seven Mountain Prayer
20. Supernatural God
21. The Snare is Broken
22. Waiting on the Faithfulness and Loving Kindness of God
23. Weapons of Mass Destruction I
24. Weapons of Mass Destruction II
25. Wisdom
26. Eliezer Lord My Helper
27. When You Pray Not If
28. Quantum Prayer Leap Decrees

ADDITIONAL BOOKS BY DR. SARAH MORGAN

1. 7 Days of Fasting and Prayer
2. 21 Days of Fasting and Prayer
3. 30 Days of Fasting and Prayer
4. Confessing the Proverbs
5. Declaring the Psalms
6. Intercession by Pattern
7. Prayer the Master Key Revised Edition
8. Sing O' Barren Revised Edition
9. Seed of a Women
10. The Prayer Factor
11. The Faith Factor
12. You Shall Decree a Thing

To Sponsor a Prayer Academy Seminar in your city, to invite Sarah Morgan to your next conference, service, encounter, Revival, Crusade, or for additional information, please contact the Prayer Academy administrative offices.

To enroll or for additional information regarding **Prayer Academy University (PAU)**, please visit www.prayeracademy.university

Contact Information:
Email: admin@prayeracademyglobal.com
Phone: 1-888-320-5622 ext.1

ABOUT THE AUTHOR

SARAH MORGAN is skillful, prolific, insightful, and balanced in the teaching of God's word and mightily used in the gifts of the Holy Spirit. Sarah Morgan is an anointed and appointed vessel of God who has shaken the community of Los Angeles and abroad. She has been honored with several awards that recognize her contributions to the community, influence in leadership, and examples of accomplishments and sacrifice for family and friends. She is the Chancellor of Prayer Academy University, and she facilitates Prayer Academy Seminars, conferences, and retreats, which serve to equip, empower and transform ministry leaders from "Doctrine to Demonstration" with the mandate to preserve the Legacy of Prayer in the church.

Sarah Morgan's ministry is sought after and has taken her to South, East and West Africa, London, and across the United States. Everywhere she goes, the power of God within her is demonstrated as the atmosphere changes in her presence, and forces in existence move back to accommodate the Word of God.